Lives and Times

Madam
C. J. Walker

M. C. Hall

Heinemann Library
Chicago, Illinois

© 2003 Heinemann Library
a division of Reed Elsevier Inc.
Chicago, Illinois

Customer Service 888-454-2279
Visit our website at www.heinemannlibrary.com

Designed by Herman Adler Design
Illustrations by Yoshi Miyake
Printed and bound by Lake Book Manufacturing

07 06 05 04 03
10 9 8 7 6 5 4 3 2 1

Library of Congress Cataloging-in-Publication Data
Hall, Margaret, 1947-
  Madam C.J. Walker / M.C. Hall.
    p. cm. -- (Lives and times)
Summary: Introduces the life of Madam C. J. Walker, who invented hair-care products for African Americans, founded factories and beauty schools, and organized one of the first national meetings of businesswomen in the United States.
Includes bibliographical references and index.
  ISBN 1-4034-3252-X (HC) -- ISBN 1-4034-4257-6 (PB)
1. Walker, C. J., Madam, 1867-1919--Juvenile literature. 2. African American women executives--Biography--Juvenile literature. 3. Cosmetics industry--United States--History--Juvenile literature. [1. Walker, C. J., Madam, 1867-1919. 2. Businesspeople. 3. African Americans--Biography. 4. Women--Biography. 5. Cosmetics industry--History.] I. Title. II. Lives and times (Des Plaines, Ill.)
  HD9970.5.C672W3543 2003
  338.7'66855'092--dc21

                                        2003001524

Acknowledgments
The author and publishers are grateful to the following for permission to reproduce copyright material:
p. 4 Hulton Archive/Getty Images; pp. 5, 7, 13 The Granger Collection, New York; pp. 6, 12, 15, 16, 18, 20, 22, 24, 27, 29 A'Lelia Bundles/Walker Family Collection; p. 9 Missouri Historical Society, St. Louis; p. 10 Corbis; p. 14 Western History Collection/Denver Public Library/#F-22925; pp. 17, 25 Schomburg Center for Research in Black Culture/New York Public Library; pp. 19, 21 Madam C.J Walker Collection/Indiana Historical Society; pp. 23, 26 The Byron Collection/Museum of the City of New York; p. 28 Janet L. Moran/Oijoy Photography

Cover photographs by Schomburg Center for Research in Black Culture/New York Public Library, The Granger Collection, New York, A'Lelia Bundles/Walker Family Collection.

Photo research by Dawn Friedman.

Special thanks to Michelle Rimsa for her comments in the preparation of this book.

Every effort has been made to contact copyright holders of any material reproduced in this book. Any omissions will be rectified in subsequent printings if notice is given to the publisher.

Some words are shown in bold, **like this.**
You can find out what they mean by looking in the glossary.

Contents

Taking Care of Hair

Hair products are used at beauty shops.

For thousands of years, people have used **products** to take care of their hair. They use these products to make hair grow faster or look nicer.

4

Different hair products are used for different kinds of hair. Madam C. J. Walker **invented** products that were made specially for the hair of African-American women.

Walker used products on her own hair, too.

The Early Years

Sarah Breedlove was born on a small **plantation** in Louisiana. Of her family in the United States, she was the first person who was not born a **slave.**

This is the cabin in which Sarah was born in 1867.

Sarah's family was very poor. The children picked cotton to help earn money. Because she had to work, Sarah did not go to school long enough to learn to read or write.

These children are working on a cotton plantation in 1870, just like Sarah did.

Moving to the City

By the time Sarah was eight years old, both of her parents had died. Sarah's older sister took care of her. The girls earned money by washing other people's clothes.

When Sarah was young, clothes had to be washed by hand.

When she was fourteen years old, Sarah got married. Her husband died six years later. Sarah and her daughter, Lelia, moved to St. Louis, Missouri, where Sarah's brothers lived.

Sarah hoped to find work in St. Louis.

Work and School

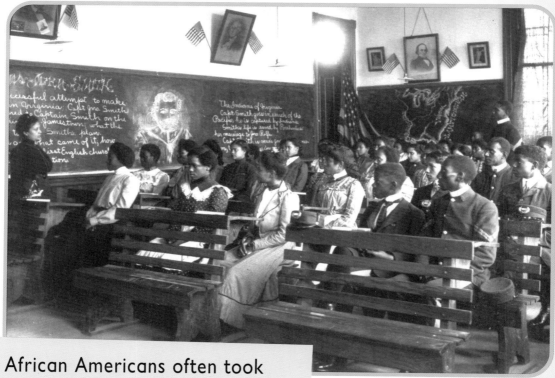

African Americans often took night classes together.

For the next eighteen years, Sarah worked hard washing clothes. She saved enough money so Lelia could go to college. Then Sarah could do something for herself. She could go to school.

At that time, many African-American women went to night school. Sarah worked all day. At night, she studied reading, writing, math, and other subjects.

Sarah worked hard to learn to read and write.

Hair Problems

Sarah was happy about going to school. But she was worried about something else. Her hair was falling out. Other African Americans had the same problem.

Sarah cut her hair short to hide how much of it was falling out.

Many African Americans were poor and did not eat a healthy **diet.** Also, few hair **products** were made for their type of hair. Sarah found some that helped. She took a job selling those products.

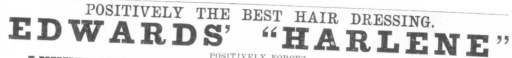

Hair products were often advertised in newspapers in the 1890s.

Becoming a Businessperson

Sarah moved to Denver, Colorado. She continued selling the hair **product** she had sold in St. Louis. She sold it to other people in her neighborhood.

Drugstores in the 1900s sold many different kinds of products, just as they do today.

Sarah told people how her products had helped her hair grow. They wanted their hair to look like Sarah's. They bought her products. Soon Sarah had a successful business in sales.

Sarah carried before and after photos to show people the quality of what she was selling.

BEFORE USING

New Products

Sarah was very happy about her success with selling the hair **product.** She decided to make her own product. She started experimenting with different **ingredients.**

She called her first product Madam Walker's Wonderful Hair Grower.

Walker soon had many products to sell.

In 1906, Sarah married an old friend, Charles J. Walker. Sarah began to call herself Madam C. J. Walker. She labeled her new hair products with her new name.

The Business Grows

Madam Walker had many ideas about how to sell things. She put **advertisements** in newspapers. She traveled around the country to show her **products** to people.

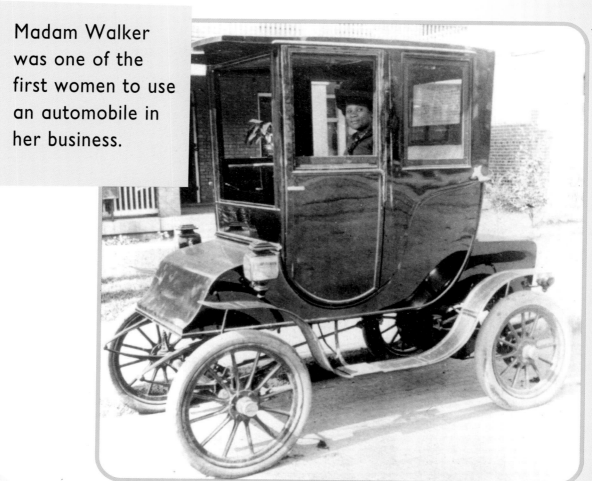

Madam Walker was one of the first women to use an automobile in her business.

Madam Walker also hired some of her **customers** to sell Walker hair products. That gave her more time to **invent** new products and think of ways to sell them.

Madam Walker trained all of her employees on how to sell her hair products.

Beauty Schools

Madam Walker wanted to give many African-American women the chance to earn money. In 1908, she opened a beauty school in Pittsburgh, Pennsylvania. Women came from all over to learn how to use and sell Walker **products.**

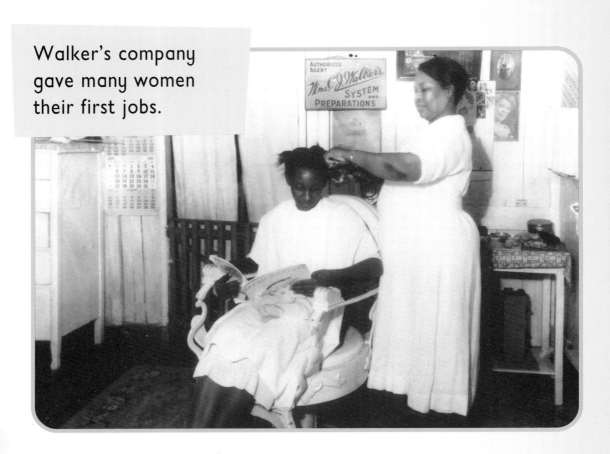

Walker's company gave many women their first jobs.

Two years later, Madam Walker moved to Indianapolis, Indiana. She built a **factory** there to make her products.

Walker's factory helped her make more of her product in less time.

Success

Madam Walker is shown here with some of her Ohio sales agents.

Madam Walker worked hard to make her company grow. She built up a strong sales team. She was a good boss. She took care of the people who worked for her.

In 1916, Madam Walker moved to New York to be near her daughter. At first she lived with her daughter. Then Madam Walker paid to have a beautiful house built. The house had 34 rooms!

Walker invited artists, writers, and other important people to visit her in her home.

Working for Others

Madam Walker wanted to help other African Americans. She gave money to help young people go to college.

Walker also gave money to people who were fighting for **equal rights.**

Madam Walker became friends with many African-American leaders. She worked with them to ask for laws that would protect African Americans. She made speeches and marched in parades.

It is thought that Madam Walker was part of the Negro Silent Protest Parade in 1917.

A Family Business

Madam C. J. Walker was the first female African American to be so successful in business. She was only 51 years old when she died in 1919. She left her company and beautiful house to her daughter.

Walker's daughter changed her name to A'Lelia. She learned how to run her mother's company.

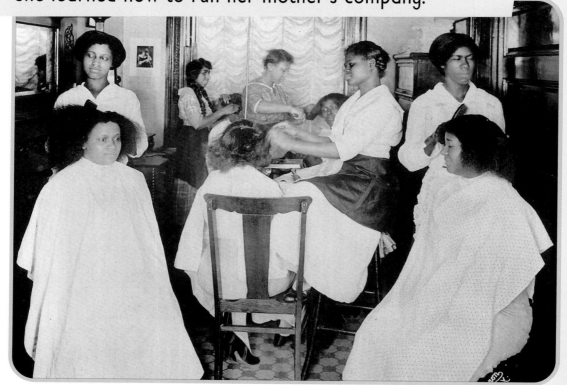

These are newly trained Walker Company saleswomen.

The company Madam Walker started was in business for another 66 years. Many African-American women became successful by working for the Walker Company.

Remembering Madam Walker

Today, an old Walker Company **factory** in Indianapolis is called the Walker Theatre Center. There is also a **museum** where people can learn about Madam Walker.

At Walker Theatre, city children take classes in dance, music, and art.

In 1998, the U.S. Postal Service printed a stamp to honor Madam C. J. Walker. People remember her for her line of hair **products.** She also made things better in the workplace for African Americans.

Madam Walker worked hard and was very successful.

Fact File

- Sarah Breedlove was born just two years after slavery ended in the United States.

- Sarah's mother, father, and older brothers and sisters were all slaves until 1865.

- Madam Walker said that the idea for her first hair product came to her in a dream.

- In 1917, Madam Walker invited all her workers to a meeting in Philadelphia. This was one of the first national meetings of businesswomen ever held in the United States.

Timeline

1867	Sarah Breedlove is born in Louisiana
1882	Sarah marries Moses McWilliams
1885	Sarah's daughter, Lelia, is born
1888	Moses McWilliams dies. Sarah and Lelia move to St. Louis
1905	Sarah moves to Denver
1906	Marries and changes her name; Starts her own business
1908	Opens a beauty school in Pittsburgh
1910	Builds a factory in Indianapolis
1916	Moves to Harlem, New York
1919	Madam C. J. Walker dies at the age of 51

Glossary

advertisement something written or said to try to get people to buy a product

customer person who buys a product or service

diet foods people eat

drugstore store that sells medicines and other products

equal rights treating all people fairly and in the same way

factory place where large amounts of a product are made

ingredients things that are put together to make a product

invent to think of a new idea or create a new product

museum place where pieces of art or things that are important parts of history are kept

plantation very large farm

product something that is made

slave person who was owned by another person and could be bought and sold

More Books to Read

Colman, Penny. *Madame C. J. Walker: Building a Business Empire.* Brookfield, Conn.: Millbrook Press, 1994.

Lasky, Kathryn. *Vision of Beauty: The Story of Sarah Breedlove Walker.* Cambridge, Mass.: Candlewick Press, 2000.

An older reader can help you with this book:
Hobkirk, Lori. *Madam C. J. Walker: Journey to Freedom.* Chanhassen, Minn.: Child's World, 2001.

Index